DUST OF UNCERTAIN JOURNEY

To Michael Glaser
With appreciation and
high hope for the
coming book —

Sincerely,
May Miller
2/6/76

ALSO BY MAY MILLER

NEGRO HISTORY IN THIRTEEN
   PLAYS (with Willis Richardson)
INTO THE CLEARING
POEMS
LYRICS OF THREE WOMEN (with
   Katie Lyle and Maude Rubin)
NOT THAT FAR
THE CLEARING AND BEYOND

Dust of Uncertain Journey

By

May Miller

LOTUS PRESS
DETROIT
1975

Copyright © 1975
By May Miller Sullivan
All rights reserved

First Edition
First Printing

LC: 75-40977
ISBN: 0-916418-05-7

Manufactured in the United States of America

Price: $3.50

LOTUS PRESS
"Flower of a New Nile"
P. O. Box 601 - College Park Station
DETROIT, MICHIGAN 48221
Phone 313 862-5696

Foreword

"At home or abroad, she is the poet with the world-view. And we see ourselves not only in the people that she chooses to portray, not only in the relationship to things that have become objects of her attention, but also in relation to nature as a point of reference for our own individual psyches."

So writes Pinkie Gordon Lane in a review of one of May Miller's earlier collections. She sees the author as a sensitive observer of "deep personal insight, of absolute unquestioning moral courage" who has "suffered the imbalances of our society" and yet retained "a grace and wholeness of spirit."

Robert Hayden comments that "May Miller writes with quiet strength, lyric intensity. She is perceptive and compassionate, a poet of humane vision."

The Washington Post calls her "a poet who strikes an authentic note of love and wrath."

It is apparent in all of these observations that May Miller possesses a rare combination of deep personal concern for humankind and the ability to express her perceptions in disciplined lyricism. At a time when the gentle murmur of love is often drowned out by the scream of wrath, we believe that it is most necessary that our quiet voices be heard.

The majority of the poems in this collection were published originally in various magazines and anthologies over a period of thirty years including 1975. In submitting her manuscript, Miss Miller stated her belief that "poetry, in a life of its own, can range a past, assess the present, and look to a future. Even in assembling the poems," she continued, " I sensed something that went beyond finite time, places, and experiences. The latter were but realities that stirred thinking which crossed all ordinary boundaries." This collection does indeed reflect the infinity of which the author spoke.

For the first publication of the majority of these poems we gratefully acknowledge <u>The American University Writer</u>, <u>The Antioch Review</u>, <u>Cafe Solo</u>, <u>Common Ground</u>, <u>Phylon</u>, <u>Essence</u>, <u>The Journal of the National Medical Association</u>, <u>The Negro History Bulletin</u>, <u>The Crisis</u>, <u>Poetry: A Magazine of Verse</u>, Energy Black South Press, The Cricket Press, The Hand and Flower Press, Linden Press, South and West, Inc., The Swallow Press, and Winthrop Publishers, Inc. (Copyright 1974).

The Editors

For John

Contents

Autumn Technique	31
Bay Craft	56
Beauty Parlor	23
Burning Bush	55
Calvary Way	14
Changing Laurels	64
Child in the Night	15
Climbers, The	59
Come Morning	24
Contour of Anticipation	41
Dark Instrument	12
Death Is Not Master	33
Direction, The	66
Don't Touch	16
Dream of Wheat, The	17
Dresden Mirror	27
Janus Grief, The	26
June Has Gone	42
Knife Edge	45
Lady of the Pigeons	21
Late Conjecture	65
Leaf Bacchanal	29
Measurement	11
Old Avowal Repeated, The	32
On the Cape	57
Other Kingdom	20

Park, U.S.A., The	18
Place in the Morning	30
Quebec Road	54
Return	43
Ring Around the Roses	44
Room, The	25
Scream, The	28
Signature in Black	38
Snow-Healed	22
Tally	46
Three Scenes for All Men	13
Tuscana	52
Twist of Time	37
Venice: First Itinerary	51
Victor Is Home, The	49
Voice Heard, The	60
Washingtonian, The	19
Weatherwise	40
Where Is the Guilt	50
Wings	58
Wrong Side of Morning, The	62

One:
A Repeated Note

MEASUREMENT

A thin repeated note strikes
Against a tuning fork
To mark man's encroachment
On the God-threatened way,
To set the hour
Of his uncertain final step.
Choose an ancient scheme:
The fractional-lengthening shadow
On the unscarred dial;
The way is none the less short.
The tune begins again.

DARK INSTRUMENT

Hold me and hear me, America,
For I am that instrument
Sprung in Africa
Tuned to this land.
Beat out my music.

Beat it out lightly.
Response comes shivering
To the hand
As when foliage leans
In wind trembling.

Beat out the lyric briskly.
Vibrations quicken to staccato
Sharp as spearheads
Thrust in bodies
Moving through the night.

Beat it out heavily,
Stroke heavily.
Passion flows deep
In the runnels of my song,
An undercurrent dark with woe.

Beat out my song steadily.
Strike deliberately with calm.
A new note could throb andante
In contrapuntal voices of men,
A rhythm caught in minors,
Echoed in tempered vessel of time.

THREE SCENES FOR ALL MEN

He knows Gethsemane;
Driven to its solitude,
Has sharpened to his need
Its awful silences.

And Golgotha —
The jeers, the colored cloak,
The long and weary way
To a storm-dark hill.

He knows the Third Day —
The faith that all unnoticed
Stayed a while
To hear him from the tomb.

CALVARY WAY

How did you feel, Mary,
Womb heavy with Christ Child,
Tasting the dust of uncertain journey?
Were you afraid?
When, winding the swaddling clothes,
You laid Him in the manger,
Were you afraid?
Could you trace nail holes
Under His curling fingers,
Thorn pricks on the forehead?
Could you trace them?

I should bear a warm brown baby,
A new dark world of wonder;
But I fear the nails that pierce the spirit,
The unseen crosses.
How did you feel, Mary,
On the road beyond the star-lit manger,
Up the hill to crucifixion?
Were you afraid?

CHILD IN THE NIGHT

I heard a child cry in the night
And saw light fill a window
Across the areaway.

Half in sleep I saw and heard,
For I was the mother bringing light,
I was the baby born of me.

I was the omniscient night
Curved to a world of need
As a pulsing instrument.

I am the edge of morning
Waking keen to myself
On a single pillow touching nothing.

DON'T TOUCH

Long we have known the terms
that race to politic lip,
how in hushed studio an artist
paints by morning light.
Unashamed we probe nerve and impulse
of a boy who in shade-deep wood
marks with wonder the veining of a leaf.

Go where the bell calls from the tower
a cause — a face — a name.
Say one has told you
words would be on the wind,
color on the walls.
But tread softly the place
where the boy sleeps,
a leaf fallen from his hand.

THE DREAM OF WHEAT

Phantoms crowd the night:
Millions of black hands reaching,
High above, an owl's eye unblinking,
A stairway burnished to copper haze —
The balustrade a descending spiral
Of torn fingers writhing.
Unnumbered rows of ripened wheat
March to greedy ovens
Returning on the belt lines
Uniform loaves of stone.

Sunlight floods the wakening
Shot through with doubting:
Who will eat?
Who go hungry?

THE PARK: U.S.A.

Clouds move over;
Everywhere is the instant new.
Write winter off;
Forget the winds that drove
Old trash to dry bushes.
The hedge turns green again.

A jay swoops low to the fountain
Spraying water-crystal notes
To a black girl's singing.
Bright April, how she sings —
As if to free some captive bird
From her green hill of memory.

On benches lovers touch —
Boys flashing passion
Like gaudy scarves,
Girls wearing theirs coyly
Like grandma's lace-edged petticoats.
Rejuvenation is the keynote here
Where the old bend over carriages
To crow at babies,
The gap of years no matter
In assurance of the sun.

THE WASHINGTONIAN

Possessed of this city, we are born
Into kinship with its people.
Eyes that looked upon
Cool magnificence of space,
The calm of marble,
And green converging on green
In long distances,
Bear their wonder to refute
Meaningless dimensions,
The Old-World facades.

The city is ours irrevocably
As pain sprouts at the edge of joy,
As grief grows large with our years.
New seeds push hard to top soil;
Logic is a grafted flower
From roots in a changeless bed.
Skeleton steel may shadow the path,
Broken stone snag the foot,
But we shall walk again
Side by side with others on the street,
Each certain of his way home.

OTHER KINGDOM

Against shadowed leaves of the ginkgo trees
Light falls fluid from arching lamps
To the street below — clear and water-green
Like a truant wave from a child's dream,

Falls upon night-prowling cars
Looming out of somewhere,
Going somewhere other,
Their monstrous eyes searching.

Above the pavement, house lamps
Edge the curtained windows;
And where newcomers widen vistas,
They look from softly-draped broader frames.

Toward these, down aisles the figures move
To pierce the anonymity of walls
Where each will trace his line
Of curving laughter and sharp-angled grief.

And below the rooms of children,
Below rooms with women at stove and sink,
The other kingdom waits — the dynasty of
                roaches,
Crisp-bodied and nervous, impatient for foray.

LADY OF THE PIGEONS

At noon from her window sill
She tosses crumbs to the alley
Following their measured plunge
With eyes caught in the net of space,
Hung in nothingness.
Silent she watches as if she herself
Were wafted food for the birds.
From roof and dome, wings whirr
And liquid scroll downward
To the feast.
As if among her guests, she is fed—
The brown pigeon on the fringe
Pecking at crumbs, devouring herself
Until the urge calls other places.
Silence falls light with calm,
Void of birds, void of self.

Later the rats will come.

SNOW-HEALED

Nothing stark remains
In the snow-healed morning street.
Voices that broke home-going peace
Last evening are silent
In the muteness of frost tongue.
No scuffed print cries nakedly
Of the whore's long waiting.
Somewhere in gray emptiness
The doorstep kiss hangs frozen;
Passion — razor lightning, hot thunder
Shot through other nights —
Lies numb on the icy heart
Dulling the edges keen to memory.

BEAUTY PARLOR

Here is fancy come home to walls,
The dream of permanence for the impermanent
Fled from fountain to cubicle
Where faucets drip and steel domes mock the
        wind.
Within glass case a lush of blooms
Packs vials and lacquered jars.
No pitiless light decries that splendor
Broken on the nonchalance of time;
Mirrors in neon haze give back a rosy image.
In a corner nest a mouse of dust and hair
Nurses at its heart a pearl.

COME MORNING

Vulnerable to the midnight knock,
To the step on rib-boned stair,
The heart pulses with the stain
That moved a blood-cursed sleep.
(Damned spot, guilty hands are wrung,
Creaking boards yet walked.)
In the facelessness of dark,
The mind revives in scarlet the secret
That broke an insane tomb to purge
Bone and name in a vengeful tarn —
Over all, echoes of the threatened child:
Next time He'll rain down fire.

You don't love me; you don't love me
From across the areaway, come morning,
Shall mean less than when bruised love plays
Night bodies narcissistic with tortured rhyme:
Tattered and torn nurse the selves all forlorn
That live in the house that fears built.
In light, power will forsake the vocal night;
The prison skull release the bond
From which only the tiger now streaks free
Blazing the callous dark,
Leaving behind the little ego cats
To whine and claw the little sins
Magnified to bright Lucifer.

Come morning, out of the East,
Harbor of faith and fiction,
Hard-packed light moves silently,
Crosses a green-veined ford,
Drives through the slatted blind
Waking to other day.

THE ROOM

The room my mother left
Hears silence settling
Like the last note of requiem
That quivers in cathedral dome
And drops to the patient floor.

Pain grips the crowding faces
Cracking their shifting masks,
Above them one face newly carved
To join others of sightless eyes
Staring across the blind years.

I feel nothing in this room;
Bodiless I ride a white-leafed wave
Which plunges and falls back
Folding me among the churned blooms
In a captive sea.

THE JANUS GRIEF

Just over that hill
A child is crying.
The child is each
In the other self
Weeping cool pebbles
Into the pool of others' grief.
We would leave him there lost
Fearing the present a jagged wound
To feed those streams
That split the closer worlds
And rust the vivid bush.

DRESDEN MIRROR

I was thinking this morning of death—
Not of the larger death
But of a boudoir accessory focused
On the private scheme of living,
How the static gives back motion,
How motion comes to immobility.
It was a Dresden mirror I handled
Inherited from one long dead
Wondering whose final touch
Would break the frozen pastoral.

THE SCREAM

I am a woman controlled.
Remember this: I never scream.
Yet I stood a form apart
Watching my other frenzied self
Beaten by words and wounds
Make in silence a mighty scream —
A scream that the wind took up
And thrust through the bars of night
Beyond all reason's final rim.

Out where the sea's last murmur dies
And the gull's cry has no sound,
Out where city voices fade,
Stilled in a lyric sleep
Where silence is its own design,
My scream hovered a ghost denied
Wanting the shape of lips.

LEAF BACCHANAL

Someone said you were dying
Under a tree.
I went to where you lay,
Leaves moving around you.
Wine glistened on the loose ones
Stirring in your hair
Like new butterflies.
Wine trickled down your body
Leaving traces star-shaped
Like the leaves and scarlet
As tribal brands.

You breathed.
Fingers clutched your face
As if to tear away a leaf
Grown large, I thought,
To cover guilt.
I turned from you
Knowing that all alone
You couldn't have stripped that tree.
Alone, you did not strip that tree.

PLACE IN THE MORNING

A silken transfer waking from sleep
To breaking light flushed
On the window sill.
Shadows separate one by one.
You go away
Beyond the spindrift neon sign
Lost in a blinding arc.
I call your name.
The wild and steely echoes
Out of where you've gone —
Wheels on concrete, grinding, shrieking —
Crisp my cries
Until the fog of the dream unwinds.
You seem returned through branches
That have shed the dark.
In the flute of the morning
You are mirrored in new sun
And I take my place there too.

AUTUMN TECHNIQUE

The crisp chill breaks
And drifting leaves go
Like scored stars to mold.
Frost threads new patterns
For the lawns burned
To a gold-edged forgetting
Where no summer echo runs
But is blunted by the blast.

Under a cold compulsion
We go hand in hand
Stripped and unquestioning
To warm at old fires
Hoping them fresh performance,
Without thought of last year
Nor of the year before that—
Without traditional memory.

THE OLD AVOWAL REPEATED

Mere senses cannot possess
The inner image, the unspoken word.
Their wavering hold has no power
To sink the inviolate.
As behind shut lid a new eye burns
I shall forever see dogwood
Curved to darkened dent
And your fingers closing slowly.
With bronze vibrated on the hour
Something more than ear
Would detect your stammering footstep.
Aged and numb I should yet feel
Your hand upon my flesh
And recreate in deadened fiber
Those seconds we singed eternity.
In whatever of living,
Of unopening dark and silence,
I should know your presence
And breathe your name.

DEATH IS NOT MASTER

I cannot let you die.
I block factual death
And its memorial apology;
Within a secret self
I build a barricade
Against the dark,
There fix you shining
In a place of sun.
No soft rain of tears dwarfs you;
Straight and desperate you walk
The corridors as before
Eclipsing the minions of grief
In their naked hours,
Gathering about your head
Scorn for the grave
In which they say you lie
Until memory glows
In that astonished quarter
Burning the night white
That would bind you in sculpture.

Two:
The Direction

THE TWIST OF TIME

There was a dinosaur
On our morning lawn.
No. That's not true,
But yesterday
We really caught
And rode one.

And here the creature is
Today a silly chicken grin
On the gasoline sign.
Grumbling we pay the new price
And drive away to talk
Of depression and inflation
And of war.

Tomorrow we'll dig once more
For bones.

SIGNATURE IN BLACK

Once the search has started,
There is no end to the seeking,
To the page-by-page scrutiny
For a signature in black.
God is a wrack in childhood
Devised by the old for young dreams,
And certitude a knife bleeding the credulous,
Healing in a forgetting moment.

The child made no distinction
That morning when roused to prayers.
God was her gaunt brown grandfather
Reading from the big black book.
She thought, being timid
And tortured by drowsiness,
He will punish me. I'm sleepy.
I don't know what he says.

Sound was impact to the girl
Going with others to evening service.
About and above them the country mask
Was punctured by stars like peep-holes
And vocal with night things.
From the far grove the church bell
Called one note: *you're chosen*
Down the wayside dark.

Later imagery turned absolute.
A presence evading mind and instrument
Haunted knight legend,
In stained glass window appeared,
Tendered the flaming cup, withdrew it
Leaving lips numb and parched,
The spirit freshly plumed
As if born of ashes after cremation.

But the woman gropes defenseless
Crying out for meaning in the closing room
And along the passages of memory
Lighted with pilgrim inns.
On other paths croakings from puffed throats
Silence alike the meek and the questioning
As streams run muddy to earth's end.

WEATHERWISE

Here's word for all
Immaculate in reason:
Not one wind dies down
Because poets rage
Against cold out of season.

CONTOUR OF ANTICIPATION

Before you burn wonder in the next thicket
Fill a basket from the fabled eve.
The carousel ride was never more real
Than in the rush of that morning
When the garish steeds were still.
The dreamed cadences of bells at rest
Move more poignantly than bronze stirred.
Ever elusive to blue-black word the rhythm
Of images running a corridor of inner violins.
Formless they are reality
Leaving a contour after the flame.

JUNE HAS GONE

Illegible the signature
June scrawled on a young sky,
Her image lost except
To those of double sight.
Brilliant wings are reduced
By jewellers' craft
To brooches worn on black.
The morning song is stilled
In the unaccented void
Of cold throats.
Dead things are dead
In the definitive wind.
The once-insurgent leaves lie
Quiet in the gullies
And green rebuttal of the firs
Does not deny petals falling
On a brass tea tray.

RETURN

A fresh blouse waits
At the new gate
Near the wood's edge,
But none can still moths
Turning in old clothes
Or silence ghosts
Among the trees
Whispering white flowers
Down the night.
Nor is there one to hold
The chameleon jewel-tone in sun
Against return to the bark.

RING AROUND THE ROSES

Find that lost child
Who in a garden
Rhymed his jingle
And the other
Down the cypress lane
Who twisted it to
"Ashes, ashes,
We all fall down."
Those words bear their echo
Deep into the wasteland.
They crash the bauble
Childhood cradles briefly
Or fuse it to a prism
That stabs the innocent
And refracts the wound.
Hush ... hush.

KNIFE EDGE

(Irish Religious Upheaval, 1969)

The uneasy birds of Ireland
Have lighted on a wall
The knife edge of which
Turns up to split the notes
That ricochet.
Here the elect are redeemed by grace;
Over there saints crowd the damned.
Lament the wall.
Lament the butchered heritage,
Lament the sad, sad birds
And their broken song.
Lament.

TALLY

We lay there drained of time,
Empty as the upper bulge of hour glass
That has let slip
The last thin feel of grit.
Up love's sheerest pinnacle
We had climbed
In rhythm tuned to rhythm;
Unbodied, clasped the peak of ice,
Bathed in molten lava,
Chorused one convulsive gasp.
Seed sped to cradling womb,
Fused with Eternity.

Lost Lucifer streaked to reality,
You counted
One — three — six.
Who votes at 'Frisco?
What the whispered word at Yalta?
Why the power?
Which the count —
One — three — six?
News type one inch tall,
Startled cry on ether wave,
Voice upon voice in marble hall
Remember Greece,
Patch quilt Poland.
One — three — six.
Somewhere in the tally lost
One item — Peace.

But leave to me his childhood sum.
One, two — Buckle my shoe
Three, four — Shut the door
Five, six — Pick up sticks.
Sprawled flattened on the twilight step
To coax the first wan sapphire out,
To dot the legion aftermath;

Then safe behind the barring door
To show the star-marked body
To the other sex,
Innocent of heaven and hell
Locked there.
One, two — Buckle my shoe.

Oh! multiply the years between
. . . . . . Seventeen, eighteen.
Too soon the downy fuzz
On cheek and chin,
The back door tryst,
The feel of power in fountain welling,
And always, ever another war waiting.
Seven seas, alien sod
Or dome so vast
That God is lost in weak conception.
The sheeted stiff
To deep sea rest,
A wooden cross
On shell-pocked field,
Or charred bones
After wings are singed.
The fountain dry
Though rains may fall.
Three, four — Shut the door.

Hold, Mr. Science passing by,
Pray let me test your wares.
Penicillin, sulfa drugs,
Blood — types 1, 2, 3, 4,
Metal limbs, plastic parts,
Glass eyes, fine muscle cords —
New life to mangled flesh,
A wonder world of walking dead.

So what? No souls for sale!
Mere life beyond the burst of shell,
Bomb, bullet, bayonet, more of hell.
Dead, man-resurrected to slight and slur,
The pitying word, the thoughtless stare,
And in the end the bitter cup.
Five, six — Pick up sticks.

Fear goads reluctant flesh
Nor stealing lassitude the power
To bind me to the couch.
No seed of mine to sprout
Cork leg, plastic arm, clutching claw.
Better to be lost in muck
And slime of sewer swirl
That yet may run a clearer stream
To lap some lonely lighthouse rock
Or green again the passing plain.

THE VICTOR GOES HOME

On top of the last burned hill
A shepherd cursed the ships
Setting sail from Ilium.
Wiser he would have known
What lay behind the vanquished
In the ashes
Was before the other going home.
The blunted years of wandering done,
A stranger the victor moves
Beside his stranger son;
As beggar walks the field
He ploughed with salt;
In a paler bed, embraces
His wife of the stricken eyes
Too long fastened on a tatter
Re-woven against time.
Often in the waking night
Down through the great hall
He hears a trundling
As of chariot wheels
And the thud of flesh
Dragged three times round.
Vainly the curtains are drawn
Against a wind from the East
Blowing cold with the despair
Of broken men and the dry-eyed women.

WHERE IS THE GUILT

At last I am acquitted
My body heavy with shame.
I dip myself in the dark river,
Wash again, and once more.
What is the mass that floats from me
Down the dark river?

I am not guilty!
I am not guilty!
I tell the white birds
Flying low over my head.
(But they're busy with each other.)
Lovers, accept me, you lovers!
I call to the pair
Swept by in a canoe's rhythm.
(No answer, no matter.
I'll never see them again.)

I return to the waters
Trampling the hollow sedges
That do not bother to answer
Even persistent winds.
Only the river responds
Promising no unholy footprint.

VENICE: FIRST ITINERARY
(St. Mark's Square, The Basilica, and the birds)

This morning we visit the pigeons,
Even smaller birds of beaten wings
As they swoop in greedy dives
To the tourists' trick of corn.
We watch them gorge and defecate
On the saint's strict marble;
In earth-bound arc circle
The woman in black come
To mumble beads to mosaics
And kneel in sun before carved stone.

It is the hour. Colossal Moors
Dwarfing men below, strike.
From towered security
Bells tell the day.
The domes reaffirm in gold
The brilliance of a shrunken grace,
And the sad fat birds eat.

Above the cathedral door
Four bronze horses poise for the race,
Their rider lost
In the broken dream of Byzantium.
Forever reared in a niche
Their phantoms ride
Out from the walls of the Tetrarchs.
Great gods of fleeting cultures,
They ride,
And the sad fat birds eat.

TUSCANA

Arma virumque cano,
We scanned arms and the man
Some Virgil days ago.
(The boys translated glibly from ponies;
The girls were afraid.)

But today I walk the Latium shore
And down through a valley
Where another conqueror moves
Straightening tangled vines
Or offering prop to a young tree.
He sings to his soil
And curses occasionally
As memory, the matriarchal wolf,
Ranges back to a glory image
Of volcanoes belching lava,
Of rivers out-racing their banks.

Surely, the fruit must reward him,
This late day master
With the tang of lemon
Bitter on his fingers;
And twilight, the old magician,
Slice clean the planes of light
That fall to his shoulders
Mauve and edged by olive leaves.

Now he will make the climb
Where houses huddle up-hill,
One close upon the other,
A procession of rooms
Bed-worn and precious.
There he will lie in love
Hoping sons to be growers;

There pray before heirloom crosses
And sleep this night
Leaving the land of his crop
A still life in the valley.

Amo — amas — amat.
I love — you love — he loves.

QUEBEC ROAD

The road at dawn
Leads through towns
Whose doors shut and grey
Are fingers laid to blatant lips.
Emerging in dim elegance
Fretwork of balconies nets
The light in filigree
As platinum settings that hold
Some dark unwilling gem.
From church front, the stone
In apostolic mold breaks
Shadows into sculptured prayer.

Wheels hum to land
Where plaster saints
Extend a hand to bless the soil;
And He on crucifix hangs tall
Above bright-bloused farmers
Early in the fields.
They come late
Who peddle native wares
At wayside stall.
Ever for the passing eye
Mary bends to Her Baby;
In glass-faced box
The pale Christ bleeds red.

BURNING BRUSH

They clear the lower land today,
Set flare against brush in the breeze.
Caught in a cone of wizard light
The reeds stand long wind-wrapped in flame.
These are the reckoning of the seasons
That vibrated in their hollows trills of children,
The breath of girls in the ancient tangle,
And the tremolo of unuttered grief.
Here the men had picnicked in summer,
Impatient with passion lay in grasses
Remembering prim gardens.

They halt the flame at the graveyard rim;
No hard brown pattern of earth,
For all her composure,
Can mold them to the like of beasts.
Forever young, the skulls of their fathers
Are locked in whispering immune to echo.
This is their patrimony: flame and rain,
And for a while blessed clear-water hours
Until the absolute chill is upon them
When the reeds in tongue of fire pass
Beyond winter's long fingers.

BAY CRAFT

In the creeping mist
Ghost witches thrust their heads
Beyond pillories and from stony mouths
Hurl the lie at piety.
And old, a secret walks roof tops
In bitter vow to lovers
Swallowed by the sea
Or lost to warmer distances.
Still the fences and churches
Survive the onslaught of snow,
Of wild winds and private fires.
Little the stranger learns
Where pines hoist dark curtains
Against intruders who chip the Rock
Too late caged in a haven.
Heard only the gulls flying shrill arcs
And wind in coves whining to cliffs
That, stark with seasons,
Drain their multi-colored clay to the shore —
All phantom voices to blend
With the unregenerate sea.

ON THE CAPE

Tomorrow, I thought, I shall come
To touch again this tall pine tree,
Hear time in needles fall.
Morning-naked against earth roots
I'll build castles
Too terrible for reality
Where each identity
Cushioned in the separate room
Plays tenant tomorrow.
When a wind in transit
Rides the final cliff
In return to the sea,
I leaning in that pale wind
Through the lens of water
Will determine myself,
With sea caps dash free.

WINGS

Swans in flight stir the dream.
One can almost hear the bird
Through the high cloud blanket
Whistling in the night
To the mate beside him
As they turned in easy flight
From the Arctic's flowering snow.
Perhaps they wished the feel of earth
And time for warmth beyond the mating
Beside a bay less bound in ice.

They knew the water way and land
Here where soft tides run free
And shoreward to the ripened sedges.
With odds unnumbered in mild concept
And crash set neat as by compass point,
The male swooped . . . .
His brightness dazzled the blind airlane
To die in cold metal thundering.
And all who rode the other wings
Went incommunicable to doom.

Details slip quietly to things forgot:
Who had emplaned that night and why;
Who will tomorrow beat their fists
Against the rigid hours.
Yet none who runs the wind
Can be freed of the thinking
That for all their skill and lovely symmetry
Man and bird streaked to one appointment
Where high above the tangled muck and wrack,
A mate circled and circled without completion.

THE CLIMBERS

All is frozen in the pass
Where rocks white-glazed
Edge the face of danger,
Where cold dead thunder
Tumbles down the heights.
Linked rope on rope
The climbers in thin air grasp
The meaning of steel far below;
Through tracery of snow, dream
The warm mirage of village lights
That dare the morning cocks.
The truth of where they are
Will melt down the crystalline conceit.
Then afraid they'll climb their mountain.

THE VOICE HEARD

Oh, the elders, the poor elders
Have lost their way
Within the cobwebbed room.
Forms embryonic, unnoticed,
More misty than first morning,
Move across the wormy floor.
Unheard a wisp of echo stirs
A dust-mouse corner.
Their dreams have stood these years
In marble centered in the square
To sing an anthem to ashes
And legendize in stone.
For old ears hear what they must;
Old eyes are strict to dimensions
By other seasons set.

    Would they want it other —
    They already so dead
    Who deny lineaments of prophecy
    In the transparency of time?

We are the young
Singing in their dying,
The image mirrored —
What they were, what we are —
Free verse, hot horns, pop art,
Rosaries of sex heavens and hells.
When the voice goes hoarse
In truths too much repeated,
We hurl obscenities at landmarks,
Crash shadows, smash icons;
As dry sticks burn,
Trample the uprooted
To tread borders
Where laurel grows.

Clear of sight, taut and fair,
We carve the straight flame
Wider than death,
More narrow than our thinking.

We race the swift,
The oh so beautiful serpent
To the magnificent moment
Of our creation and absolution.
No guilt bequeathed,
No innocence applauded,
We pace the length of divinity
Bitterly brief against the night
Which is but morning twisted.
We go nowhere perhaps
Beyond the monolith of self,
Not that it matters really
As long as we come in free
In the resurrection.

THE WRONG SIDE OF THE MORNING

We wake on the wrong side of the morning
From a nightmare of wings
And mushrooms of huge death.
Weep for us whose lives are caged
In concrete, for our straw images
Seen through glass walls
Are you and you tomorrow.
Weep for yourselves then
Dismayed by that vouchsafed you.
Cry down the gods of science
Dedicated to eternity for walls
While denying youth its prophecy.

They are the idle rosy with words
That look where once a light burned
And reiterate tomorrow, tomorrow;
The dead will rise again;
Some appointed star may rekindle
The ash heap and the broken.
They prate to lull one another
And deceive you . . . Look.
Their eyes are glass eyes of teddy bears;
Their voices those of last year's snow men.

We know, we know
Though we speak in no tongue of fire
And beg no absolution,
Yet warn the stranger to this hour
Beyond a time of anger.
Weep a misshapen future
And the antic place where heights stood
Now so terribly crashed and fragmented.
Here will the hoped-for progeny range
Seeking a green sill
Where unsmiling they only scuff
Dead leaves before splintered doors.

CHANGING LAURELS

Though the crow flies an immaculate way,
Time deadheads without conclusion.
No decorum through the years remains
Implicit in fixed place.
Legend-doubting we await from N.I.H.
Typed reports to sustain or deny
The Jesus three-day life suspension.
Storied heroes who were titans
In this career or that plummet
One by one from the blazoning top
Leaving no finite word:
Who did or did not climb the hill and why.
Others go swaggering down a hall of wind
Or freeze starless in a night of ice.
It is suspect that time shall ever alter this.

A LATE CONJECTURE

Look to the end of the garden
To the scarecrow sticks
Against the stained wall like a cross.
In this tell-tale light
Trace on those limbs nicks and burns
Such as dug by heels in agony
Trying to escape.

Beyond the garden and the hour
Of broken bough and rusted fruit,
Think the legend voice
That must be crying:
What is this thing I do?
Perhaps I'd best climb down.

THE DIRECTION

Around, around,
All directions go around.
On our way to another place
We meet ourselves coming back.
Within the ends the means are self.
Even as the predatory beast adapts
To his golden flash
The camouflage of leaf and grass
We sift all points to our need,
The depth and ceiling one
Wherein naked and visible
We stand before bleak mirrors.
          Behold the image.

There was a flood;
There was an ark.
Let none deny it.
In spite of bird and spring branch,
The lie is the new season,
For no one truly forgives.
          Resist the memory.

They are believers in miracles
Who balance hours on pinpoints,
Who rivet shadows in song.
We slay our poets:
The old we reduce to absurdity,
The young we sell to skeptics.
The mighty keep their separate way
Tethering great eagles to bear arrows—
E pluribus unum.
A fish in every mound makes green;
Delirium cankers the air of cities;
Rot and red ruin corrode the dawn.
Money is made round to roll.
          Let it roll.

So are we heir to that, cursed and starred,
Which cries out for fulfillment:
Water, flame, ash in turn.
Yet fragments of asteroids exploded
Move in old restricted orbits
And do not clutter the universe.
          A shabby victory of sorts.

ABOUT THE AUTHOR

May Miller was born and educated in Washington, D.C. A graduate of Howard University, she has studied further at American and Columbia universities. The author, Mrs. John Sullivan in private life, is a former teacher of speech and dramatics at Frederick Douglass High School in Baltimore.

Miss Miller has read her poetry and served as panelist at many leading institutions and galleries across the nation, as well as in her native city where she has also participated in radio broadcasting at American University. Her readings have included many visits to public schools.

In 1972 she recorded for the Library of Congress Collection of Poets Reading Their Own Work, and she gave readings for the D.C. Bicentennial celebrations in 1973 and 1974.

Under the auspices of Friends of the Arts in the public schools of the city, Miss Miller worked for three years as coordinator for performing poets. Presently she is a member of the District of Columbia Commission on the Arts and serves as chairperson of the literature panel.

In addition to her volumes of poetry, May Miller's work has appeared frequently in such anthologies and publications as *Poetry: A Magazine of Verse*, *The Crisis*, *The Antioch Review*, and *Essence*.